The Countries
Ethiopia

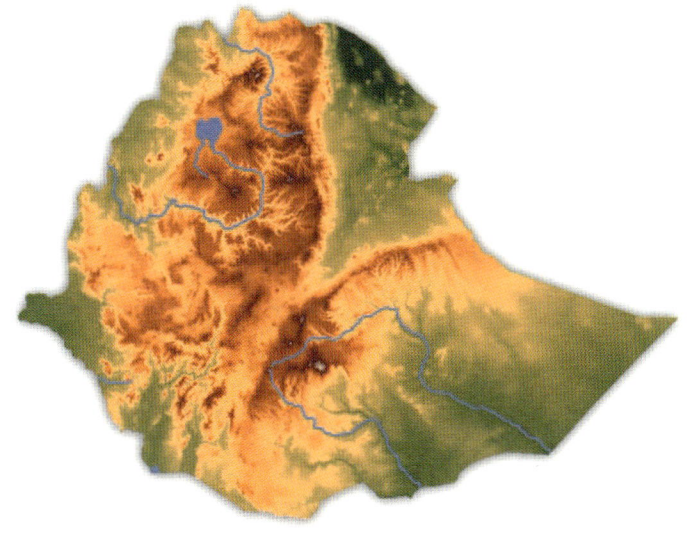

Tamara L. Britton
ABDO Publishing Company

visit us at
www.abdopub.com

Published by ABDO Publishing Company, 4940 Viking Drive, Edina, Minnesota 55435. Copyright © 2002 by Abdo Consulting Group, Inc. International copyrights reserved in all countries. No part of this book may be reproduced in any form without written permission from the publisher.

Printed in the United States.

Photo Credits: Corbis
Art Direction & Maps: Neil Klinepier

Library of Congress Cataloging-in-Publication Data

Britton, Tamara L., 1963-
 Ethiopia / Tamara L. Britton.
   p. cm. -- (The countries)
 Includes index.
Summary: An introduction to the history, geography, plants and animals, government, economy, cities and transportation, people, and social life and customs of Ethiopia, a country in eastern Africa where people have lived for millions of years.
 ISBN 1-57765-757-8
  1. Ethiopia--Juvenile literature. [1. Ethiopia.] I. Title. II. Series.

DT373 .B69 2002
963--dc21

2001045850

Contents

Selam! 4
Fast Facts 6
Timeline 7
History 8
Land 14
Plants & Animals 18
Government 20
Economy 22
Cities 24
Transportation 26
Ethiopians 28
Holidays 34
Sports & Leisure 36
Glossary 38
Web Sites 39
Index 40

Selam!

Hello from Ethiopia! Ethiopia is a country in eastern Africa. Its land contains highlands and lowlands. This land provides **habitats** for many different plants and animals. Some of Ethiopia's animals live no place else on Earth.

Some of Ethiopia's people live in beautiful cities, but most live in rural areas. Many work as farmers. Others manufacture goods or work in service or tourism industries.

Ethiopia has had several governments. Emperors and military leaders have ruled the land. Today, Ethiopia's government is a **federal republic**. The people elect their leaders. These leaders are working with the people to make Ethiopia a great place to work and live.

Selam! 5

Selam from Ethiopia!

Fast Facts

OFFICIAL NAME: Federal Democratic Republic of Ethiopia
CAPITAL: Addis Ababa

LAND
- Mountain Range: Simien Mountains
- Highest Point: Ras Dashen 15,157 feet (4,620 m)
- Major Rivers: Blue Nile, Tekeze
- Lakes: Tana, Langano, Abiyata, Shala
- Deserts: Denakil Plain

PEOPLE
- Population: 65,891,874 (2002 est.)
- Major Cities: Addis Ababa, Dire Dawa, Gonder
- Official Language: Amharic
- Religion: Ethiopian Orthodox, Islam, animist

GOVERNMENT
- Form: Federal republic
- Head of State: President
- Head of Government: Prime minister
- Legislature: Bicameral parliament
- Flag: Green, yellow, and red horizontal stripes with a yellow star on a blue disk in the center. Yellow rays streak between the star points.
- National Anthem: "Whedefit Gesgeshi Woude Henate Ethiopia" ("March Forward, Dear Mother Ethiopia, Bloom and Flourish")
- Nationhood: 1855

ECONOMY
- Agricultural Products: Coffee, cereal grains, sugarcane, potatoes; cows, sheep, goats
- Mining Products: Gold
- Manufactured Products: Leather, processed foods, beverages, textiles, chemicals, cement
- Money: Birr (1 birr =100 cents)

Ethiopia's flag

Ethiopia's money

Timeline

8000 to 6000 B.C.	Agriculture develops in Ethiopia
A.D. 100s	Migrants from southern Arabia come to Ethiopia
300s	Aksums are introduced to Christianity
900s	Islamic peoples invade Aksum
1000s	Zagwe dynasty rules Ethiopia
1300s	The capital is moved and named after King Lalibela; Yekuno Amlak overthrows the Zagwe dynasty
1527	Islamic invaders attack Ethiopia
1889	Emperor Menelik II signs a treaty with Italy
1896	Ethiopians defeat the Italians at the Battle of Adwa
1935	Italian forces invade Ethiopia
1936	Italy annexes Ethiopia
1941	Emperor Haile Selassie invades Ethiopia; Italy surrenders
1955	A new constitution is written
1963	The Organization of African Unity is formed
1974	Ethiopian military takes over the government
Late 1970s	Many Ethiopian states rebel against the government
1991	The Ethiopian People's Revolutionary Democratic Front (EPRDF) removes Mengistu from power; the Derg collapses; the EPRDF takes over the government
1995	Ethiopia holds democratic elections
2000	The people elect legislators

History

People have called the land that is now Ethiopia home for millions of years. In 1974, **archaeologists** found a human skeleton that was more than three million years old. Many people believe this means that human population began in Ethiopia.

Between 8000 and 6000 B.C., agriculture developed in Ethiopia. Around 2000 B.C., cereal grains and the plow were brought from Sudan.

Around the second century A.D., **migrants** to Ethiopia from southern Arabia influenced what became the kingdom of Aksum. The Aksums had a strong **economy**. They traded with communities in Sudan and along the Nile River and Red Sea.

The Aksums were introduced to Christianity in the fourth century. In the 900s, Islamic peoples invaded Aksum. When the Muslims broke up the Aksum kingdom, it slowly declined.

Ruins at Aksum, the ancient capital of Ethiopia

In the eleventh century, the Zagwe **dynasty** ruled Ethiopia. The capital was moved and later named after King Lalibela in the thirteenth century. During Lalibela's reign, the people carved 11 stone churches out of red tufa rock. Many people consider the churches to be great contributions to African **architecture**.

Later in the thirteenth century, Yekuno Amlak overthrew the Zagwe dynasty. Then in 1527, Islamic invaders attacked again. The Ethiopians joined the Portuguese to defeat them. During the nineteenth century, Western European countries colonized many African countries. But the Ethiopians defeated European attempts to colonize their country.

A church carved out of red tufa rock

In 1889, Emperor Menelik II signed a treaty with Italy. It gave Italians permission to rule Eritrea. But the Italians tried to conquer all of Ethiopia. On March 1, 1896, the Ethiopians defeated the Italians at the Battle of Adwa.

A coin showing Emperor Menelik II

Italian forces invaded Ethiopia again in 1935. In 1936, Italy **annexed** Ethiopia. Emperor Haile Selassie went into exile. He organized forces and invaded Ethiopia in 1941. On January 20, Italy surrendered.

Ethiopia enjoyed many stable years. The government developed an education system. In 1955, the Ethiopians wrote a new **constitution**. The Organization of African Unity was formed on May 25, 1963.

In 1974, Eritreans rebelled against Ethiopian rule. **Famines** in Tigray and Welo killed many Ethiopians. On September 12, 1974, the military took over the government.

Colonel Mengistu Haile Mariam

The military government was called the Derg. Lieutenant Colonel Mengistu Haile Mariam led the group. The Derg suspended the **constitution**. It also broke up the **parliament**. Many Ethiopians were killed for protesting.

In the late 1970s, many Ethiopian states rebelled against the government. **Famine** and drought affected millions and killed thousands of people. In May 1991, the Ethiopian People's Revolutionary Democratic Front (EPRDF) removed Mengistu from power.

The Derg government collapsed and the EPRDF took over. It wanted a multiparty government. Meles Zenawi was named temporary president. In August 1995, Ethiopia held **democratic** elections. Zenawi was elected Ethiopia's **prime minister**. Negasso Gidada was elected president. In May 2000, the people elected **legislators**.

Meles Zenawi

Ethiopians are strengthening their democratic government. But they have much to do to repair the Derg's damage to their country. The Ethiopian people are working together to make Ethiopia a great place to live and work.

Land

Ethiopia is a flat land with two high **plateaus** in the middle. The plateaus divide Ethiopia into highlands and lowlands. The Great Rift Valley divides the plateaus into eastern and western. The Awash River flows through the valley. The Blue Nile starts in Ethiopia.

The North Central Massifs dominate the Western Highlands. The range's highest mountain is Mount Ras Dashen. It is 15,157 feet (4,620 m) high. This is Ethiopia's highest point. The Blue Nile, Baro, and the Tekeze Rivers run through the Western Lowlands. It is very hot here. So, few people live in this region.

In the Eastern Highlands, Mount Batu is 14,127 feet (4,306 m) high. The Shebele and the Genale Rivers flow through the Eastern Lowlands.

The Ethiopian Plateau

Land 15

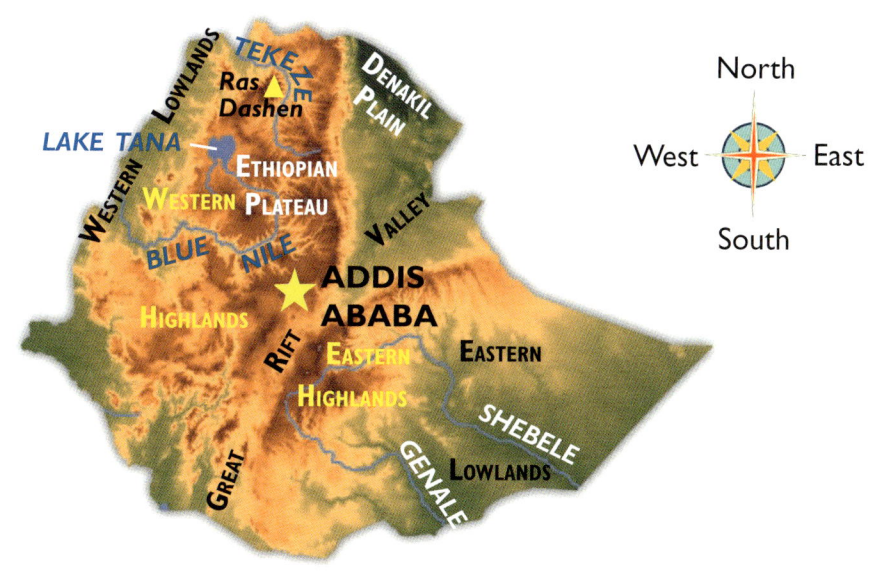

In the Great Rift Valley, the Denakil Plain dips as low as 380 feet (116 m) below sea level at a **depression** called the Kobar Sink. This is the lowest point in Ethiopia. The plain is very hot, and there is not much rain. The Ethiopian Lakes Region is also in the Great Rift Valley. This is one of Ethiopia's most settled parts.

Tisissat Falls on the Blue Nile

Land 17

Rain

Rainfall
AVERAGE YEARLY RAINFALL

Inches		Centimeters
Under 10		Under 25
10 - 30		25 - 75
30 - 60		75 - 150

Temperature
AVERAGE TEMPERATURE

Fahrenheit		Celsius
80° - 90°		27° - 32°
70° - 80°		21° - 27°
60° - 70°		16° - 21°
50° - 60°		10° - 16°

North
West   East
South

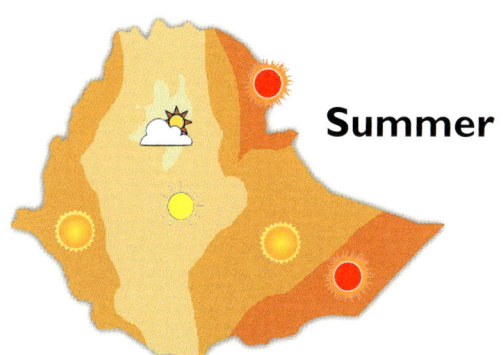
Summer

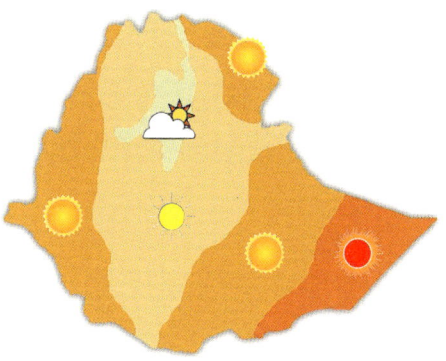
Winter

Plants & Animals

Ethiopia's varied land makes it home to many different plants and animals. Forests cover part of southwestern Ethiopia. Eucalyptus trees are common in these forests. They were imported from Australia in the 1890s. Coffee and *teff* originated in southwest Ethiopia.

Many animals are native to Ethiopia. The Walia ibex is a wild goat. It lives in the Simien Mountains National Park. Its red-brown coat has black stripes on the front of each leg. Walia ibexes have long, black horns.

The Simien jackal, or Ethiopian wolf, is another of Ethiopia's native animals. Its coat is mostly yellow. But its throat, neck, and chest are white. The Simien jackal weighs about 40 pounds (18 kg). It lives on the Ethiopian **Plateau**.

The Walia ibex and the Simien jackal are endangered animals. People are taking over their natural **habitats**. So there is less room for the animals to live. And their food supply is becoming scarce.

Jackals, wild dogs, and foxes are abundant in Ethiopia. There are lions, elephants, leopards, zebras, giraffes, and rhinoceroses, too. But these animals are not as common.

The Ethiopian government is working to protect its natural resources. Ethiopia has 20 national parks and **sanctuaries**. They total more than 21,000 sq. mi. (54,400 sq. km). Here, Ethiopia's plants and animals can live long and prosper without human interference.

A eucalyptus tree

Government

Ethiopia is a **federal democratic republic**. It is governed by the **constitution** of 1994. Ethiopia's federal government is divided into **executive**, **legislative**, and **judicial** branches.

The president and **prime minister** hold executive power. The president is head of state. He or she is elected by the House of People's Representatives. The president serves for six years and can serve two terms.

The prime minister is elected by the legislature. The prime minister is the head of government, and commander-in-chief of the armed forces. The term of service is five years.

The legislative branch contains the **parliament**. It has two houses: the House of People's Representatives and the House of **Federation**. The House of People's Representatives has 548 members. The members are elected by the people. The House of Federation has

Government

108 members. They represent the nine regions in the **federation**. All **parliament** members serve for five years.

The **judicial** branch is the **Federal** Supreme Court. The House of People's Representatives appoints the president and vice president of the Federal Supreme Court. The State Supreme Court hears state cases. The State Council appoints the president and vice president of the State Supreme Court.

Lieutenant Girma Wolde-Giorgis (center) is sworn in as president after being elected by the parliament in 2001.

Economy

Most Ethiopians work as farmers. They grow corn, barley, wheat, **millet**, *teff*, **sorghum**, and sugarcane. Coffee is Ethiopia's main export crop.

Ethiopians manufacture food products, **textiles**, leather goods, tobacco, and chemicals. Ethiopia exports coffee, hides, **legumes**, and oilseeds. Imports are machinery, **petroleum** and petroleum products, metal, food, and animals.

Energy is produced by firewood and charcoal. But most of Ethiopia's power comes from **hydroelectric** plants on rivers.

An Ethiopian woman in traditional dress pounds dried coffee beans into powder.

Economy 23

Two men work together to harvest teff, a grain unique to Ethiopia and an important staple crop.

Cities

Addis Ababa is Ethiopia's capital and largest city. About 2 million people live there. It is the headquarters of the United Nations **Economic Commission** for Africa and the Organization for African Unity. It is connected to all **provinces** by highways. Addis Ababa's railroad connects it with the port city of Djibouti in the country also called Djibouti. The capital's chief industries are leather **tanning**, cement, breweries, and textile mills.

Many people visit the Emperor's palace and **parliament** buildings in Addis Ababa. Addis Ababa University, technical schools, and the National Library are there, too.

Africa Hall, the headquarters of the United Nations Economic Commission for Africa and the Organization for African Unity

Dire Dawa is Ethiopia's second-largest city. Highways connect it to Addis Ababa, Harer, and Djibouti city. Dire Dawans manufacture textiles, cement, and food products.

Another of Ethiopia's important cities is Gonder. From the seventeenth to the nineteenth centuries, it was Ethiopia's capital. It is famous for its many castles and churches. Many people visit and admire the fine **architecture**. The Public Health College of Haile Selassie I University is in Gonder.

Guzara Palace in Gonder

Transportation

Addis Ababa is linked to all of Ethiopia's **provinces** by highway. The city is also linked by roads to Nairobi, Kenya, and by railway to the port city of Djibouti. Ethiopia once had access to the Eritrean ports of Aseb and Mitsiwa. But this access no longer exists.

Ethiopia has three international airports. The largest is Bole International Airport, near Addis Ababa. Travelers may fly between Ethiopian cities. There are also flights to countries in Africa, Europe, and Asia. Ethiopian Airlines is the national air carrier.

Cars and buses at the Mercato, one of Africa's largest open-air markets

Transportation

Ethiopian Airlines' Boeing 767 in flight

Ethiopians

A young Amhara girl

Many **cultures** make up Ethiopia's people. The Amhara make up Ethiopia's largest **ethnic** group. Most live in the north and central parts of the country. The Oromo live in the eastern and southern parts of the country. Other groups are the Tigre, Afar, Somali, Saho, and Agew peoples.

About 100 languages are spoken in Ethiopia. Amharic is the national language. Oromo, Tigrinya, and Amharic are the most commonly spoken.

Most Ethiopians practice the Ethiopian Orthodox religion. It is a Christian religion. Other religions in Ethiopia include Islam, Judaism, and animism.

The Ethiopian family unit usually consists of parents and children. In the cities, families live in large apartment buildings. They wear clothes similar to those American and European families wear.

Injera

3/4 cup teff flour
3 1/2 cups water
salt to taste

Mix teff flour and water in a deep bowl. Let stand at room temperature about three days until it bubbles. Stir in salt to taste. Cook over medium heat on a greased skillet like pancakes.

AN IMPORTANT NOTE TO THE CHEF: Always have an adult help with the preparation and cooking of food. Never use kitchen utensils or appliances without adult permission and supervision.

English	Amharic
Yes	Awo
No	Aye
Thank You	Amessagganalehugn
Please	Ibakkwon
Hello	Selam
Goodbye	Dehna huna

LANGUAGE

The traditional Ethiopian clothing is called a *shamma*. A *shamma* is a white cotton dress. It sometimes has a colorful border around the edge of the fabric. Both men and women wear *shammas*. People who live in the country wear brightly colored *shammas*, and clothing made from leather.

Ethiopian education includes elementary schools, junior and senior secondary schools, universities, and technical schools.

An Ethiopian classroom

People 31

An elderly Ethiopian man wearing a shamma

Ethiopia's national food is *injera*. *Injera* is flat, pancake-like bread made from *teff* flour. *Teff* is a grain that contains more iron than wheat or barley. *Teff* contains yeast that causes the *injera* bread to rise. Ethiopians use *injera* to scoop up a sauce called *wot*. *Wot* is often spicy and sometimes contains meat and vegetables.

A young boy harvesting teff

A Dorze woman cooks injera, *a part of the national Ethiopian dish* injera *and* wot.

Holidays

Timkat is the most important holiday in Ethiopia. Timkat is three days long, beginning on January 19. It celebrates the **baptism** of Jesus Christ. The first day they have a huge feast. On the second day, they celebrate the baptism. On the third day, they hold the Feast of St. Michael.

Ethiopians celebrate Enkutatash on September 11. Meaning the "Gift of Jewels," Enkutatash celebrates New Year's Day and the feast of St. John the Baptist. There's dancing and singing in every village.

Meskel is another important holiday. Meskel is also called Finding of the True Cross. It is celebrated on September 27. This holiday honors the discovery of the cross Jesus was **crucified** on.

An adorned deacon holds a ceremonial cross for Timkat Festival.

Sports & Leisure

Ethiopian athletes participated in their first Olympic games in 1956. Since then, the country has won 13 medals, all in track and field events.

Many Ethiopian athletes participate in long-distance running. Fatuma Roba is the first African woman to win an Olympic gold medal in the marathon competition. She won the gold medal at the 1996 games in Atlanta, Georgia.

Haile Gebrselassie has won the world championship in the 10,000-meter event three times. He won the Olympic gold medal in the 10,000-meter race in 1996. He holds many world records. In 1998, he was named IAAF Athlete of the Year.

Soccer is a popular sport in Ethiopia. The Ethiopian Football **Federation** was founded in 1943. The first Ethiopian Cup match was held in 1945.

Afwerk Tekle is a famous Ethiopian artist. He designed the beautiful stained glass window at the United Nations **Economic Commission** for Africa headquarters. Other famous Ethiopian artists include Makonnen Endalkaches, Kebede Mikael, and Telke Tsodeq Makuria.

Fatuma Roba

Glossary

annex - to add land to a nation.
archaeologist - a person who studies the remains of people and activities from ancient times.
architecture - the art of planning and designing buildings.
baptism - a Christian ceremony marked by ritual use of water to admit the baptized person to the Christian community.
commission - a group of people chosen to perform certain duties.
constitution - the laws that govern a country.
crucify - to put to death by nailing or binding the wrists or hands and feet to a cross.
culture - the customs, arts, and tools of a nation or people at a certain time.
democracy - a governmental system in which the people vote on how to run the country.
dynasty - a series of rulers who belong to the same family.
economy - the way a colony, city, state or nation uses its money, goods, and natural resources.
ethnic - a way to describe a group of people who have the same race, nationality, or culture.
executive - the branch of a government that puts laws into effect.
famine - an extreme scarcity of food.
federal - the central government of a country.
federation - a union between states or nations.
habitat - a place where a living thing is naturally found.
hydroelectricity - the kind of electricity produced by water-powered generators.
judicial - the branch of a government that administers the laws.
legislative - the branch of a government that makes laws.
legume - the fruit or seed of leguminous plants (as peas or beans) used for food.
migrant - a person who moves from one place to settle in another.

millet - a grass cultivated for its grain, which is used for food.
parliament - the highest lawmaking body of some governments.
petroleum - a thick, yellowish-black oil. It is the source of gasoline.
plateau - a raised area of flat land.
prime minister - the highest-ranked member of some governments.
province - one of the main divisions of a country.
republic - a form of government in which authority rests with voting citizens and is carried out by elected officials such as a parliament.
sanctuary - a refuge for wildlife where predators are controlled and hunting is illegal.
sorghum - any of a group of tall, tropical grasses grown for grain, syrup, and fodder.
tan - to make a hide into leather by soaking it in a special liquid.

Web Sites

The Ethiopian Embassy
http://ethiopianembassy.org
Learn about Ethiopia's history, people, and culture at the official site of the Ethiopian Embassy in Washington, D.C. Don't see the answer to your question? Ask the Ethiopian Ambassador!

Department of African Studies
http://www.sas.upenn.edu/african_studies/country_specific/ethiopia.html
This site from the University of Pennsylvania has information about Ethiopia and also some great links.

These sites are subject to change. Go to your favorite search engine and type in Ethiopia for more sites.

Index

A
agriculture 4, 8, 22, 32
Aksum 8, 10
Amlak, Yekuno 10
animals 4, 18, 19
Arabs 8
architecture 10, 25
arts 37
Awash River 14

B
Baro River 14
Blue Nile River 14

C
children 28
cities 4, 24, 25, 26, 28
clothing 28, 30
constitution 11, 12, 20
crops 8, 22, 32

D
Denakil Plain 16
Derg 12, 13
Djibouti 24, 25, 26

E
Eastern Highlands 14
Eastern Lowlands 14
economy 8, 22
education 11, 24, 30
Endalkaches, Makonnen (artist) 37
energy 22
Eritrea 11, 26
Ethiopian Lakes Region 16
Ethiopian Plateau 19
Europeans 10

F
family 28
food 19, 22, 32

G
Gebrselassie, Haile (athlete) 36
Genale River 14
Gidada, Negasso 13
government 4, 11, 12, 13, 19, 20, 21, 24
Great Rift Valley 14, 16

H
history 8, 10, 11, 12, 13
holidays 34

I
industry 4, 22, 24, 25
Italians 11

K
Kenya 26

L
Lalibela (king) 10
land 4, 14, 16, 18, 19
language 28

M
Makuria, Telke Tsodeq (artist) 37
manufacturing 4, 22, 25
Mariam, Mengistu Haile (lieutenant colonel) 12
Menelik II (emperor) 11
Mikael, Kebede (artist) 37
Mount Batu 14

N
national parks 19
Nile River 8
North Central Massifs 14

O
Olympic games 36

P
plants 4, 18, 19
Portuguese 10

R
Ras Dashen (mountain) 14
Red Sea 8
religion 8, 10, 28, 34
Roba, Fatuma (athlete) 36

S
sanctuaries 19
Selassie, Haile (emperor) 11
Shebele River 14
Simien jackal 18, 19
Simien Mountains National Park 18
sports 36
Sudan 8

T
Tekeze River 14
Tekle, Afwerk (artist) 37
transportation 24, 26

W
Walia ibex 18, 19
Western Highlands 14
Western Lowlands 14

Z
Zagwe dynasty 10
Zenawi, Meles 13

SEP - 1 2009
2421

DISCARD